Pusheen™ COLORING BOOK

Claire Belton

GALLERY BOOKS

New York London Toronto Sydney New Delhi

GALLERY BOOKS
An Imprint of Simon & Schuster, Inc.
1230 Avenue of the Americas
New York, NY 10020

Copyright © 2016 by Pusheen Corp.

This Gallery Books trade paperback edition May 2019

GALLERY BOOKS and colophon are registered trademarks of Simon & Schuster, Inc.

For information about special discounts for bulk purchases,
please contact Simon & Schuster Special Sales at 1-866-506-1949
or business@simonandschuster.com.

The Simon & Schuster Speakers Bureau can bring authors to your live event.
For more information or to book an event, contact the Simon & Schuster Speakers Bureau
at 1-866-248-3049 or visit our website at www.simonspeakers.com.

Manufactured in the United States of America

17 19 20 18

ISBN 978-1-5011-6476-7

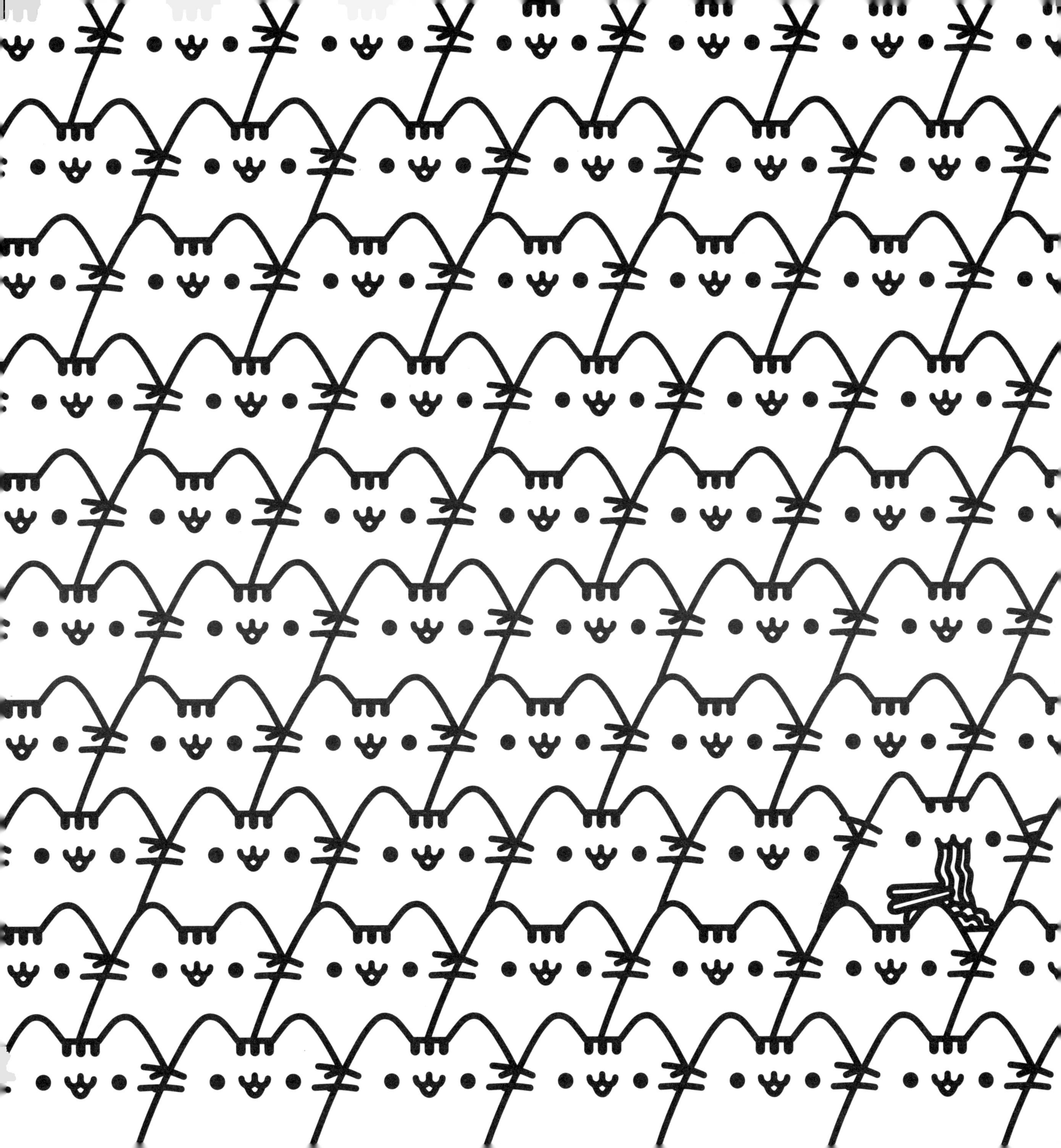

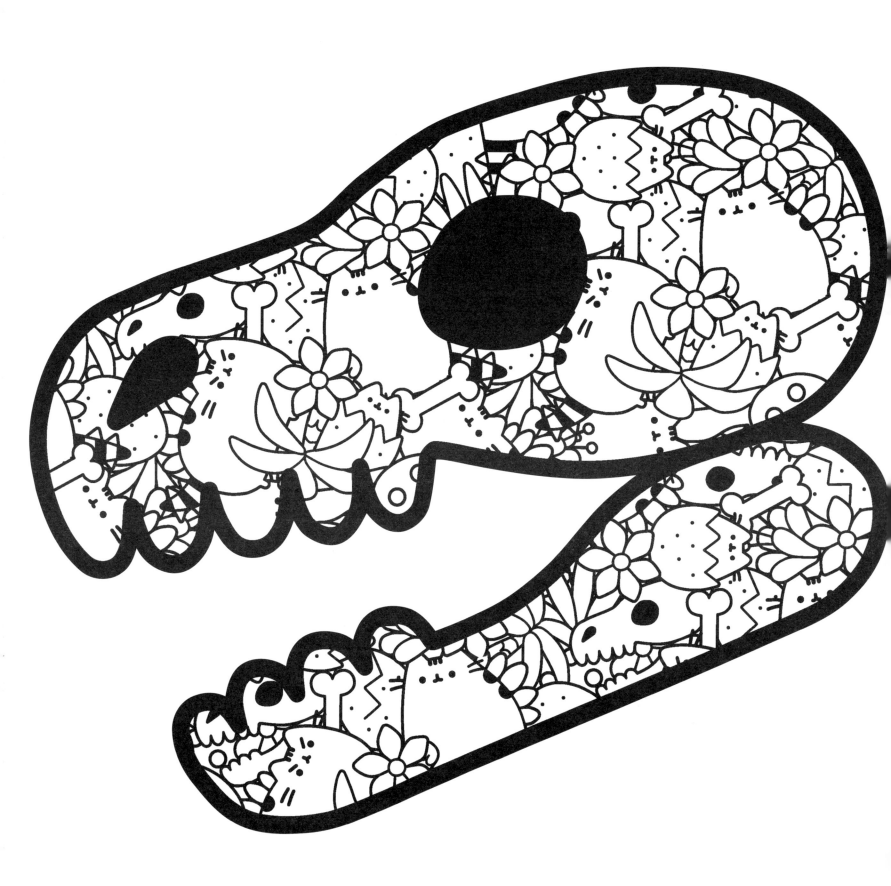

Pusheen's guide to being fancy

Not fancy

Kind of fancy?

Fancy

Super fancy

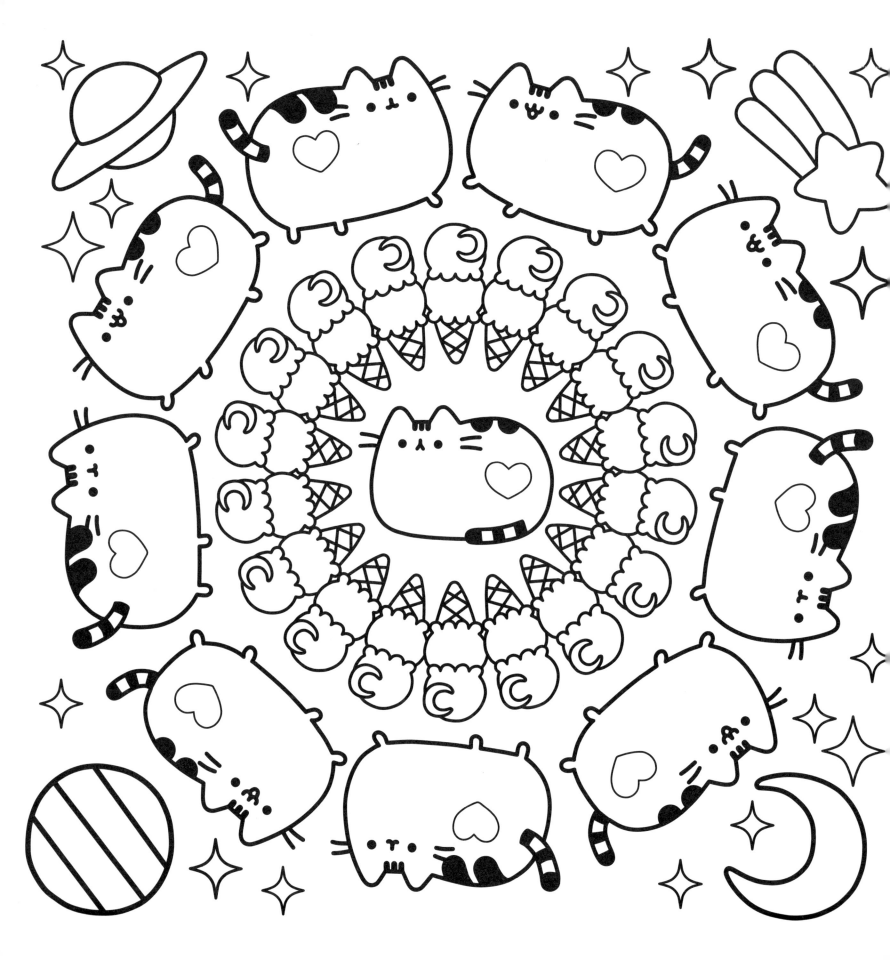

Let's Bake!

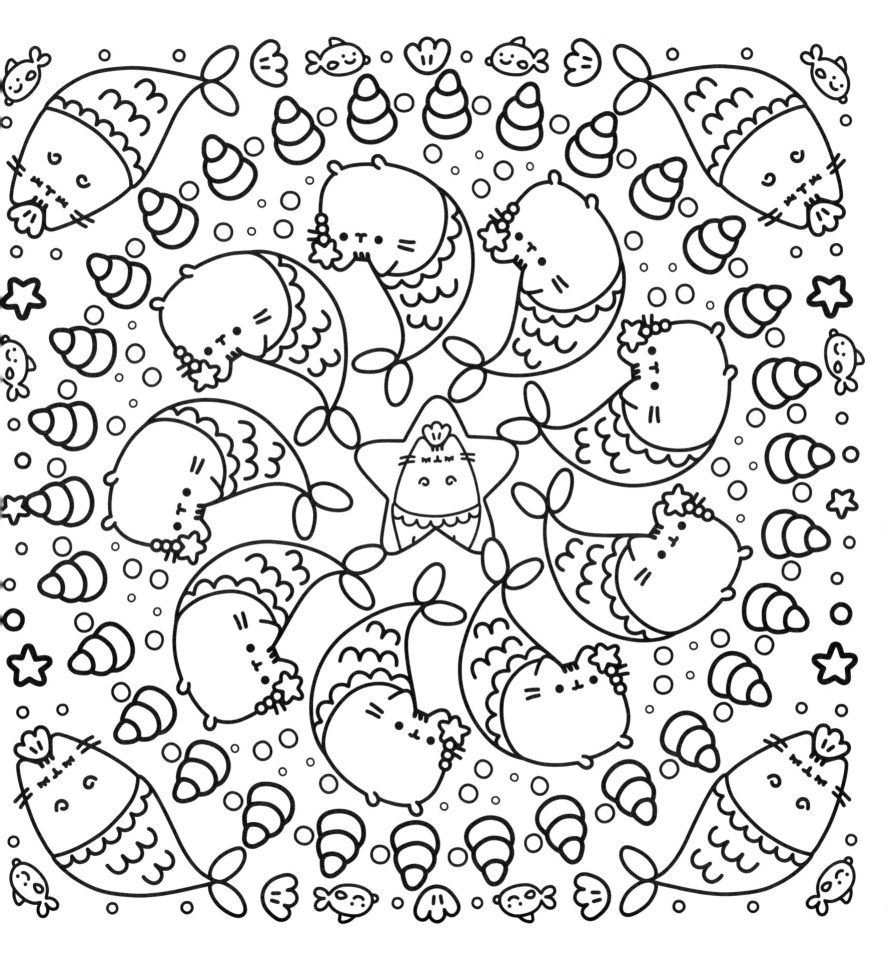

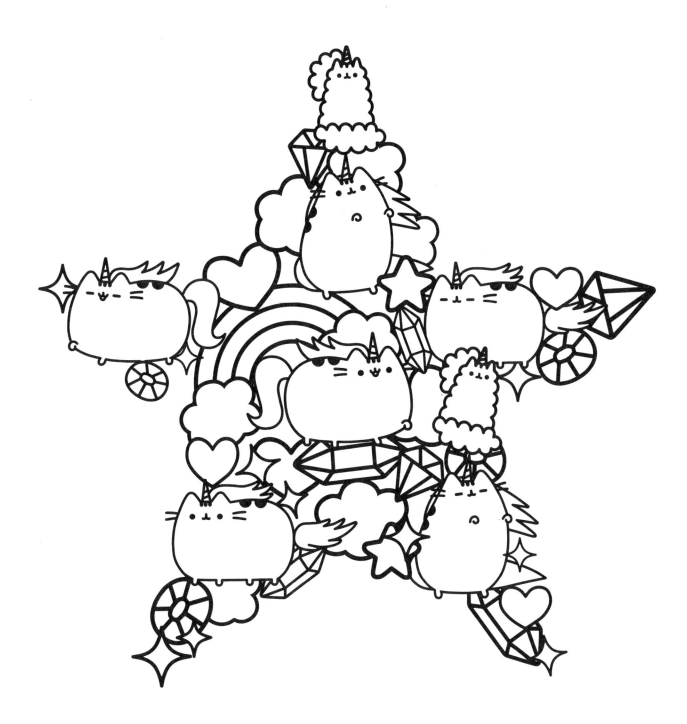

Spring

Winter

I love kitties!

Places that cats belong

The sink: No

Your shoes: No

The table: No

Your bag: No

This thing: ???

Your heart: Yes

TRICK
OR
TREAT

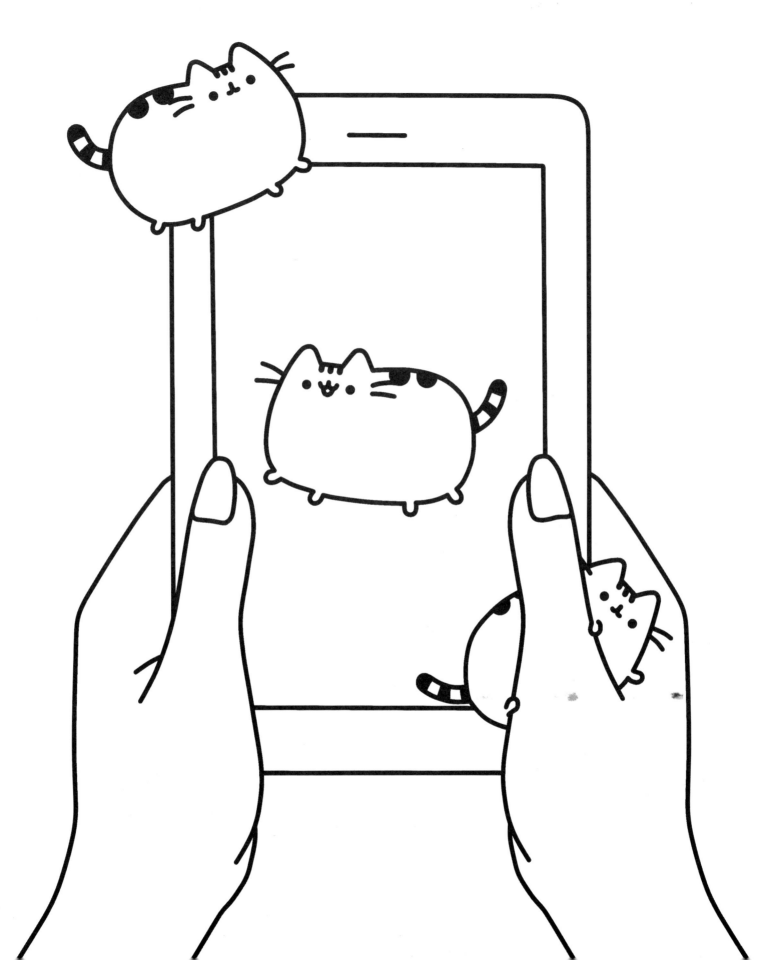